Affirmation

Selected Poems: 1986—2006

First published in 2007 by
The Dedalus Press
13 Moyclare Road
Baldoyle
Dublin 13
Ireland

www.dedaluspress.com

ISBN 978 1 904556 65 7

Dedalus Press titles are represented in North America
by Syracuse University Press, Inc., 621 Skytop Road,
Suite 110, Syracuse, New York 13244, and in the UK by
Central Books, 99 Wallis Road, London E9 5LN.

Printed and bound in the UK by Lightning Source,
6 Precedent Drive, Rooksley, Milton Keynes MK13 8PR, UK.

Cover image: 'The Letter that Nevere Arrived'
© Jannis Psychopedis

The Dedalus Press receives financial assistance from
An Chomhairle Ealaíon / The Arts Council, Ireland.

Affirmation

Selected Poems: 1986—2006

Haris Vlavianos

Translated from the Greek by
Mina Karavanta

Foreword by Michael Longley

For Katerina

O, du Geliebte meiner siebenundzwanzig Sinne,
   ich liebe dir!—
Du deiner dich dir, ich dir, du mir.

—Kurt Schwitters

Contents

Foreword

seek the reasons
for which you name
something beautiful
and the peculiar grammar
of the word beautiful
will unconceal itself to you

The lines I have chosen as an epigraph come from Haris Vlavianos's 'Contemplating the Object'. He is a philosophical poet who ventures down what he calls "the dark alleys of metaphysics". He seeks "the fleece of perfect form" or, in another of his formulations, "the exquisite poem of the genuine". He wants to be "reconciled with the perpetual music of concepts." He is drawn not only to the world's surfaces and the difficulties of describing and explaining them ("the constellation of objects"), but also to what might be read between the lines of a poem and even in the white spaces that surround it. In 'The Poem of an Other Poetics', for instance,

> The words however
> keep falling –
> snowflakes of a real life
> in the margins of the poem.

And in 'Silence' the poet confesses:

> How many times have I thought I had managed
> To hang on to a verse,

> While in reality
> I was already in the margin of a page,
> Under erasure by my very own presence.

He often mentions "reality". It is easy to forget what a strange abstraction "reality" is, suggesting as it does both materiality and truth. Is this, in Vlavianos's lines, the "reality" that T. S. Eliot means when he says "Human kind / Cannot bear very much reality"? Or is it closer to the Wallace Stevens of *Adagia:* "The ultimate value is reality"? Or is it both? (In the above quotation, of course, "in reality" might be conveyed colloquially as "in fact" or "in truth".) In 'Temperate Memory' Vlavianos does indeed talk, perhaps impatiently, of "...reality / that continually updated data bank". Only imagination can accommodate the "data bank", and the mother of imagination is memory. Throughout his work Vlavianos vigorously examines this classical aesthetic:

> It was not the heliotrope in the vase
> but the odourless flower in his memory's hollow
> that emitted this pure aroma.

Objects and specific details are transformed by the poet's invention and become possessions of the mind, properties in a poem, as in 'Our Face':

> The rustling of leaves
> (the turning of the page)
> brings you back to the place you have chosen
> for this refined ritual:
> walnut sideboards, Tiffany lights,
> Victorian desks . . .

Again and again in these poems presence implies absence and vice versa ("erasure by my very own presence", as we have already seen), so that

Whatever is gone
Is saved in us
As that which is gone.

The poet mysteriously suggests: "The absence of love always has the same face". Who is present and who has gone away? "[T]his is all about her voice," the poet declares at the beginning of 'Pentimento': "Any other metaphor would be destined for ruin." Is it a lover, is it the muse, "the beautiful woman / and her thundering voice"? Is it poetry, the poem itself? 'Our Face' closes with a lovely movement and what seems to me one of the finest lines in this collection:

The vase is full of chrysanthemums.
This enlightening gesture has no end.
Perhaps an angel looks like what we have not forgotten.

The recurring antithesis between presence and absence generates an obsessive imagery of whiteness and silence: the moon, snow, unmarked paper, bed sheets, "a white paradise / of all possibilities"; "white light like snow in the room"; "the whiteness of the first image". These lines from 'Silence' could be read as a kind of motto for the entire collection:

white roses
amidst white stones
beneath a full-moon sky
reminiscing about you
and the soft snow
that covered us

The atmosphere of many of the poems has an amorous, even erotic shimmer. "Come: let us lower the blinds, / let us lie on the white, starched sheet." The poet's lover acts as a representative of the muse: she could be her embodiment. Several episodes are shadowed by sexual jealousy, when the woman is remembered "in the arms of the

man whom for months / she secretly met at the café of Vigna Clara".
Even the happier encounters feel fragile and provisional:

> when the wind abated
> she turned her face to his side
> she smiled
> pulled the sheet softly
> up to her eyes
>
> (he caught a look of the mole
> in her right armpit)

With this poet emotional and aesthetic answers can be glimpsed
only out of the corner of the eye, in the margins. In *Minima Poetica*
Vlavianos writes that "Even the most complete poem is nothing but
a fragment." The length and intensity of his obsession with language
has produced "fragments" which work like tesserae in a mosaic.
Somehow they marry and merge, and the picture is realised: "The
leaf of reality. / The exquisite poem of the genuine."

MICHAEL LONGLEY

I

The Diary of a Poem

An Evening without an Eve

I

Carefully watch
the objects around you
(flowers, books, pictures),
watch them
as they sluggishly swing
in their metaphysical innocence.

You are not certain that they exist
yet you must go on
watching them
till the end of your time.
"It is a question of faith from now on."

When does a familiar, rainy place,
a particular scenery,
change into a new thought?
When does an intimate sound
(of oars cutting the river in two)
become a strange melody in our mind?

Someone turns on the light.
Someone fears the dark—
the sigh of autumn leaves—
the mirror games of memory.

Whatever is gone
is saved in us
as that which is gone.

"The daisies you hold in your hands
are not the daisies your hands are holding."
They are dust.
Words that try to become the meaning
of this predestined gesture.

Of this necessary but vain gesture.

II

Another arrow always follows Zeno's arrow:
that which pierces and slices it in two.

So we wither away alone in our *glorious* present
as the day slowly, casually progresses to its end.

You will shut your eyes
and begin to dream of your exotic refuge:

the place where a new, precious life
is treasured for you.

Can you take such a reward?
So much generosity?

Her name is still configured in the wind.

Affirmation

When will you say
                              yes
when will you let the passion of those days
                              (February 1990 absolute reassurance
                              in the gaze   the smile   the first
                                          embarrassed gestures)
possess you again?

You can still hear her voice.
          No, you can still remember her.

                    What is not real
(the reflection of the face on the water
the hand that suddenly rose
to draw the circle of valediction)
                    should look real.

What never was
should be again.

The mind
in a perpetual rotation
invents the words that you will utter
(you will offer)   at the right moment.

Beauty is not the question now.
Maybe it never was.
Nor is the pace (not even the rhythm)
                    of today's confession:
to say I love you is to say I want you to be

Emotions
(fear   guilt   grief   rage
                    are you trapped in the whiteness of the first
                                                            image?)

are swiftly disguised in lines
            lines extracted from a conceivable body. (Unreal)

So?

Lines: (We need to move on   I am still on your side)

The gods will not return   (they never left)
            *
Is everything expended?   Let us begin to live
            *
To be able to write: I have been happy for an
                                                    entire day.

            *
He has lost everything.   Even loneliness.

                                    And history?

To bow to necessity
                    or to the accidental?   (of the plot)

(to the necessity of the accidental?)
and history?

                    with skill cut
right where freedom
            "is clothed in the cloak of responsibility."
                                    (Responsibility of the one
                                        who stirs the ashes

who ceaselessly speaks
who asks for absolution   devotion   love)
                                                      (submission?)

Which image of the world
          are you trying to re-construct?

(Which pronouncement (vision) continues to be incomplete?)

Ingenuous metaphors
          harmonious alliterations
                    thoughts that attend to the panting of language

So?

          and history?

the woman who hides
her eyes under the veil   (mistress?
for how long?)

(is she looking at you?   at others?   at her past?)

                    ... at the moment

when someone takes the chair away   (last chance)
and the music begins again
                              the moment
you reach out
          to hold on to the void
and

Contemplating the Object

there must be objects
if the world is to have an unalterable form

> (the most beautiful
> is the object that does not
> exist)

objects, the unalterable
and the subsistent are one and the same

> (mark the point
> where the object stood
> and no longer is
>
> it will be
> genuine mourning
> for its beautiful absence)

objects are what is unalterable and subsistent
their configuration is what is changing

> (now you have an empty
> space
> prettier
> than the object
> prettier
> than the place forsaken by
>
> a white paradise
> of all possibilities)

the configuration of objects
produces states of affairs

    (vertical lightning
    strikes the barren horizon)

in a state of affairs
objects stand in a determinate relation to one another
the determinate way in which the objects are connected
is the structure of the state of affairs

    (form is
    the possibility of structure)

the structure of a fact
consists of the structures
of states of affairs

    (the totality of existing
    states of affairs is the world)

the image is the fact

    (it is the unmade world
    that jostles at
    the gates of your canvas)

abide by the intimations
of your inward eye

that which the image represents is its essence
its truth lies in the concurrence
of its essence with reality

    (remove the poem—
    the object

from the reveries
of the inward eye)

place in the empty space
a square thought
add to the concept of imagination
the concept of order

(seek the reasons
why you name
something beautiful
and the peculiar grammar
of the word beautiful
will unconceal itself to you

this object surrounds you
inscribes you
contains you
describe it   now)

The Poem of an Other Poetics

[*Variation*]

After Wallace Stevens

I

Clear water in a glistening vase.
Yellow and red roses.
White light like snow in the room.
Fresh snow (the end of winter)
softly falling on the invented place.
The afternoons are returning without sounds,
without secrets, without impatient faces.
Round vase.
Porcelain painted with roses.
Yellow and red.
The water—unruffled emptiness.

II

And still the water,
the snow,
once were enough to compose
a new whiteness—
more necessary than the meaning of flowers
blooming inside the cool memory of happiness.
(Your ecstatic gaze
confirms that imagination
can lay bare the memory again and again).

III

The mind seeks to escape.
This thought
(the possibility of the specific metaphor)
has been exhausted.
The roses, the vase, did not exist.
They do not exist.
The words, however,
keep falling—
snowflakes of a real life
in the margins of the poem.

The Archaeology of a Morning

Yet, the days are more bearable.
From a point on
      there is no return.
That point was the end
and all the delays were not signs of indecision
but symptoms of a thwarted heart.

Neither the nuptial spring
and the sweet courtesan's agreeable chant
nor the rose-petals soaked in tears
and the wind-blazed fingers.
Neither "blessed is He who comes"
nor "distressed is He who follows".

Rain inside
      and outside.
Nature's morbid release
and loss of colour
bringing me back to harshness.
Behind the blossomed bougainvillea
the lovers, wanted in the dark,
are savoring pleasure.
The words inured by the anticipation
of the belated night
emerge from the body
with the violence dictated by
the tender transparency
of the foreseen setting.
Behind the bougainvillea
behind the cries of the gratified flesh
fertility's revenge on life.

The absence of love always has the same face.
I would like to cry for you
believer in the icon of your heart
but the vanity of a bare chest
is not enough to keep the blood running.

There is no fair end.
There is nothing
not even a make-believe Eden to mourn.
Let's sing the throbbing bodies
while gazing out to the deep sea's brimming tranquillity
let's sing the fading éclat
let's sing
for words are no more made up
than what they make.

Who?

Mis-echoing Blanchot

I come to light the minute I posit myself as a question.
This question—
not the one with your angst or doubts,
constantly besetting you as you wrote—
is now present
lying silent between my lines
patiently awaiting the one
who will attempt to solve it.
The question
(now posited in your absence)
is addressed to me
and is made of words
transformed, as if by magic,
into art.

The attention I show to myself
can be considered morbid narcissism.
Yet I defend my honour
by eternally questioning it.
I assert myself through an interrogation
that often leads to my disgrace.
My story is nothing but the chronicle of this interrogation.

The question cannot be answered
for, once posited,
it automatically becomes an accusation
against my means and ends.
My kingdom is built on my ruins.
If I have any power
I derive it directly from
this endless process of annihilation and re-creation.

Every poem that asks for a place in my history
has to tell it anew
in ways not yet known.
If my past has to assume its existence,
my future is to have it in store.
But who can claim that he knows the future?
You?

Temperate Memory

It was not the heliotrope in the vase
but the odourless flower in his memory's hollow
that emitted this pure aroma.
The flower did not reveal any of the secrets
that the sunflower—in its touchable complacency—
shamelessly admitted,
nor could it anyway by its nature
claim what, however little or much, a presence
                                        might pronounce.

The idea of the flower
was not conducive to a vivid recollection;
on the contrary,
its beauty,
that is, the plenitude of its amorphous being,
in truth had something clear and final.

Something inside him told him
that reality—
this continually updated data bank—
is nothing but a genuine invention,
the need to deny the image
that with such certainty your eyes reflect.

Unwritten

On a theme by Williams

I strive;
strive in every way to salvage this "wonderful experience",
to transform it (for my own needs, too)
into a convenient, subdued memory.
"Out of the air in the coldest room
imagination can fashion the warmest passions," you write.
If only you knew
with what devices poetry manages—
for the sake of this imagination—
to displace life,
to reduce it to a simple matter,
to discolor our every radiant word,
so that the most benign avowal
seems affected and contrived,
if only you could see,
even for a moment,
the light cast upon your beloved Aphrodite
by two eyes swifter and more passionate
than the painter's hands,
would you see why this poem—
and no other—
can speak of us,
can speak of you,
can never be you,
for, though the day is coming to its close,
we have to pretend
that our life is beginning now,
that this last kiss is our first.

Vous Êtes plus Beaux que Vous ne Pensiez

For Kenneth Koch, εις μνήμην

Whatever we have written
will one day be used against us
or against those we loved
since poems cannot
(as we well know
or eventually learned)
exist outside words
and observe life
and its melodramatic episodes—
especially those that involve us—
through the dazzled eyes of a stranger,
the stranger now holding you
                          in his arms
and through your broken voice
whispering:

"If Paradise
is a meadow strewn
with yellow and red roses
(bowing as you glide through
to your beauty)
then these kisses
and all the night kisses
are real
for only something as real
as love
can die
and be resurrected—
in a day."

19

Silence

A

White roses
amidst white stones
beneath a full-moon sky
reminiscing of you
and the soft snow
that covered us.

("I have no ties," you'd told her, "nor roots",
knowing that every word makes its own land.)

E

"The word of farewell—
a rival, fervent *adieu*—
does not ponder on what is gone
but only on what is to follow," you wrote,
ending your letter with the phrase:
"Grey is rougher than black;
it contains some light,
the hope that when we open our eyes
we'll still be here."

H

The gains of a denial
that continues to avow
in the name of love:
"we speak to break our loneliness;

we write to suspend it," you said
as you sent back her letter—
unopened.

I

I write with eyes lowered
but with eyes that behold
her light within them:
there is only one light,
as there is only one poem.

O

How many times have I thought I'd managed
to hang onto a verse,
while in reality
I was already in the margin of a page,
under erasure by my very presence.

This poem is my face;
the face you loved.
I erase it with slow, steady strokes.

Stay. Listen.
You'll meet me where words
(with the frayed threads of a cancelled promise)
shape the colourful web of my silence.
Where lyricism bows
to the relentless reality of the design.

The night, every night,
conceals a "rosy dawn".

Whatever dies within us
always dies with us.

Υ

We live on this bank.
We die on the other.
Yet the river flows
in our black-eyed mind.

There is a source—
and a destiny.
And our passion's burning eyes
constantly changing colors
as we unclench the words.

The poem is written
not upon water,
but of water.
For water.

"I'm in love," you said
and wept before her.

Ω

You kissed her last wish
and vanished into the dream—
of the poem.

[Note: "A", "E", "H", "I", "O" & "Ω" are the seven
vowels of the Greek alphabet.]

The Veil

A man locked in a labyrinth
    does not seek truth
        but his Ariadne.

Truth is not an unveiling
    that destroys the secret;
        it is the un-concealment that does it justice.

Our experience remains the captive of knowledge
    that no longer is our experience;
our knowledge is trivialized by an experience
    that has not yet become knowledge.

We must weave new poetic paths
    that will designate the potential places of a "truth"
neither true   nor false
a truth that will be
    implausible
        improbable
            impossible
thereby making error   (*pathos*)
    the thread of our life.

II

In the Arcades (of History)

The Angel of History

Angels are not of this
But of another world that knows no pity.
Nothing disturbs the everlasting bliss,
And while man dies they sing their alien ditty.
—Demetrios Kapetanakis, "Angel"

They need no faith
in Heaven and Hell
nor play "hide and seek"
in the dark alleys of metaphysics
nor of course yield the palm
while seeking the fleece of perfect form.
They have other priorities,
other needs,
another view in the end.
("Key-phrase")
They watch,
observe,
know when the crucial moment comes
how to fix their gaze,
their piercing ecstatic gaze
on the image of life
("which one, I wonder?")
and—*click*—
to imprint all of its glow
onto a shiny, colour snapshot,
in which beside the—*click*—beers, cigarettes, lighter,
beside the—*click*—
glossy magazine
beside the—*click*—sunscreens, lotions, mobile,
you can discern
("with a little effort...")

the lusty, windswept bodies of young lovers—
for what else does the way the man's head
tenderly leaning on the woman's belly mean—
and in the back behind the bougainvillea
a renovated windmill
"that *naturellement* comfortably sleeps six or eight at most".

But perhaps it's a bit too late for all this,
I mean late for this kind of bitter, ironic humming and hawing—
even statements—
where your glorious,
meaningful past
(your words)
conflicts with their dry, dreary present
(your words again),
since you know, better than I,
that it isn't easy to escape
with a "but what's more important is to…",
"the circumstances dictate that…";
I certainly prefer in my free time—
which, just between us, is not that free—
to read Marianne Moore's *Blessed is the Man*
"than to…"
(analyze the impasses of relativism).
Still: if indeed
"blessed is the man"
who "does not denigrate, depreciate, denunciate",
"does not rationalize, retreat, equivocate",
who knows
"that egomania is not a duty",
who favours "difference, query, tolerance",
who "does not acquiesce, does not adjust",
then who truly among us is the one
who can say,
or rather cry, so everyone will hear him,

(even those inside your yuppie windmill)
"Yes, I am that man,
I am the chosen one
who has come not to bring Peace
but the Sword."
Who?
No one, I would say,
and I think you would agree.
So, back to square one.
Or, if not exactly square one,
somewhere close to that.
Certainly there are gradations, hierarchies,
we cannot level everything.
We will not let *the rubbish* choke us to death!
Yet, Eurydice would have disappeared into the dark
even if Orpheus had not turned to look at her.
That is the nature of things—
and let's not open that chapter now
on the ritual of preordained movements,
on the gazes that never meet.
Orpheus should (as an artist)
have known that,
have known that life is a continuously
repeated *memento mori*
in which everything comes to be
in the confined time of our conscience.

Surely, there is no point
in insisting on those matters any longer.
The sea stretches infinitely before our eyes
and the sun is at its highest point in the sky.
Come: let us lower the blinds,
let us lie on the white, starched sheet.
We too need a little sleep.
History can wait.

August Meditations

1.

If a man in his forties
is still drawing seas and dovecotes,
if in his thought is reflected
a sun more transparent,
more lucid than the sun of reality,
if the word "Amorgos" is not just
the mask of a fleeting, adolescent memory,
then between the poem of desire
and the poem of necessity
real loss is throbbing.

2.

Prologues have been consumed.
They cannot always substitute the topic.
He must decide whether he can
hold on to this absolute idea
even if he has ceased to believe in its power.

3.

Successive metamorphoses of paradise.
The eye tries to interpret the enigma of beauty
while Delos is slowly emerging on the horizon.
Summer feels like an eternity.
The poem begins to invent itself
the moment he turns his face to the light.

(The moment the imagination,
freed from the sensation of the blazing white,
vertically rises in the sky.)

4.

Not one sail on the horizon
tearing the canvas apart.
The image of a tree
with its wind-swept boughs scavenging the ground
is not a part of the scenery today.
Yet, the old lady, creeping uphill on her knees,
tightly holding her icon, is.

5.

The man is walking on the beach alone.
He is still touched by the melodious whisper of the waves,
the way the water is persistently lulling the rock to sleep.
Nature around him
(cedars, rotten fishing boats, shingles)
has a melancholic, unaffected brightness.
If he were to die at this moment,
he would want to be here,
in this place, where he has been before.
Even for a while.
For now.

Hotel Insomnia

It is... easy to be certain. One has only to be sufficiently vague.
—C.S. Pierce, *Collected Papers*

at night
        with the full moon of contradictions
                shining on the dome of your mind

you are thinking of changing roles
        of finally taking off the mask of grief

yesterday
                enchanted by the possibilities of your feelings you
                                                        wrote:

only love as passion has meaning,
every profound spirit needs a mask—
thus the subtlety of its embarrassment demands

today
        under this predictable sky
                you want to think
        that the avenue stretching at your feet
ends somewhere—
        to a final resolution of the matter
                to a synopsis that will allow you to stand in awe of
the predestined unfolding of the story

        your story—

in whose dramatic episodes
　　　you seek to recognise the beckoning of affirmation
　　　　　the assurance of reward

the light is glaring
"the light is always glaring"

it is late though
to leaf through the moment　　　　　　　　　　(life is not an argument)

no one feels like reading any more
neither do you　　　　　　　　　　　　　　　(let the texts speak)
who, exhausted by the intensity
of the last hours,
pick up the phone

"a double espresso"

(as always the best sleeping pill)

Pascal's Will

For Jorie Graham, για την οφειλή

I

The eye languidly
learns to illumine the invisible,
exerts itself to see things
when their essence flees,
when, withdrawn from their temporary form,
they lose the (holy) aura of presence.

II

Just before he closed his eyes
he asked his sister
to stitch inside his coat's lining,
(without even looking at it),
the note that contained
the "incontestable proof
                    of God's existence",
convinced that upon opening it
he would see His merciful,

                                        almighty face.

III

The glacial figure of the philosopher
impressed upon his sister's gaze,
(we can visualise the scene,
the space where it unravels),

34

and the forsaken—forever now—
content of its last-minute thought.

IV

The night casually spreading
on his lifeless body
has aptly interpreted
his last wish:
not as the need
of a self-centred believer
eager to disclose the truth
that he has just invented,
but as the desire
to hand over to the progeny
the void letter
of a dignifying,
profoundly human gesture.

V

The inevitable knowledge of a new reality.
And the mind that now rests
(reconciled with the perpetual music of concepts)
inside its ethereal creations.
The vindication of the thinker that alone,
without the blessings of the spectres,
has brought the world to the measures
of his own annihilation.

Autumnal Refrain

Following a lead by Stevens

When the last leaves have fallen,
we shall return at last to our familiar, intimate place,
to this cherished sanctuary
our fatigued body has left unfulfilled
for the necessities of inevitable knowledge.

It is difficult, almost impossible,
to choose even the adjective
that would lend some meaning
to this bare coldness,
this causeless grief
that spreads gradually, steadily,
eroding your life's innermost recesses.
A simple, natural gesture
might be the first step,
the beginning of a new attempt.
If not now, not today,
tomorrow without fail.

Lack of imagination?
That too will have to be invented, naturally;
and the stage will be set
as the instructions on the paper demand.
The stone house must be kept erect.
The arch in the front room
(your precious, priceless past), especially this.
And the old lintel with the mermaid.
And the fig tree in the garden, and the oleanders,
and the dry stonewall, all must remain.

All.
That the ruin, the rift, the absence may be revealed.
That the strife, the fall, the work may be appraised.

The autumnal wind
that gave these words their body,
fiercely effacing their metaphysical gleam,
knows all too well the secret they conceal.
As do you
who stoop to lift a dry leaf from your doorstep.
The leaf of reality.
The exquisite poem of the genuine.

Sonnet

I thought that if I could include it all,
if I could find the way to speak exhaustively of such matters—
albeit vaguely—
I would be once and for all done with them
and would have the chance finally to give myself
to something else, less errant;
then again I thought
it would be preferable, maybe,
(and more true to my *real* intentions)
to follow the exactly reverse tactic
and remove almost everything from the narrative.
I thus began to chop, write off,
(I have a talent for that)
slowly at first,
ferociously then,
anything I considered redundant—
I confess that everything seemed to be so
as I was moving along—
and pretty soon I was left
with some wrenched words and phrases

> (*In the zoo, in Rome, I had my picture taken riding the lama*
> *divorce, court cases,*
> > *when suddenly I saw her in the arms of this*
> > *strange man*)

that naturally meant nothing to you
or to anyone for that matter.

Yet, they meant something to me;
I had written them
and for some reason—
don't ask me what—
I had kept them;
so they were real.
Meanwhile the truth moved on, of course,
and vanished behind the mountains,
but left something in its wake,
call it if you may "nostalgia for the cypresses"
or the "Janus-faced spring",
it doesn't matter,
or rather it does, but only for the one who now
drives down the steep dirt track to your house
and suddenly
("a dog must have leapt in front of him")
loses control of the wheel
and crashes into the rock.

It was all a nightmare, naturally.
But life is all about that, right?
Like it or not
we've learnt our lesson well;
we've reached the age of knowledge (fear),
we cannot plead ignorance
(we've already lost a dozen friends or so)
so let each one close his notebook
and for one day allow
the beasts of his garden to run freely
in the verdant, paper meadows of his memory.

It's a national holiday today
and the guards have the day off.

De Imagine Mundi

For John Ashbery, φίλος

*"How beautiful, how unexpectedly sweet life would be
if we were not forced to live it..."*

Once, things were different.
The messages that times bore with them
were part of an absolute truth;
the looks, the gestures, the trivial talk
meant something,
the errant signs,
these too with their lurking conceit confirmed
that love was something more
than just a game of longing.

A clear sky
or a handsome man
poring over a Greek manuscript
(metaphors invented to contain us)
can not engrave your face in my memory

can not colour the charted space
with the precision this recollection's shadow
demands.

I ask for more;
much more.
A living context that can accept me,
a density of light that can reveal
imagination's true possibilities,
a specific language whose subtle command
can endow that dazzle with the depth of your beauty.

What power can check the gallop
of the deformed dream plunging over the horizon,
what will can interpret this decisive
                                        gesture
that interprets nothing?

The day comes to its end.
We have to stay here.
In this silvery daze

        the soul grounds itself.

Esthétique de la Beauté

For Vaso Kindi

Je hais le mouvement qui déplace les lignes,
Et jamais je ne pleure et jamais je ne ris.
—Charles Baudelaire, "La Beauté"

At the *trattoria* across the *Palazzo Ducale*,
he is now sitting alone
at the very same table   (where so many years ago),
having his lunch with a glass of *Brunello* (her choice),
taking the same route, inversely.

Pain is certainly human.
Yet beneath the present 'no'
lurks a passion for a 'yes' that has never been quenched.
The book he is holding in his hands
(an old edition of Cavalcanti's sonnets)
confirms this: the paradise of that forsaken faith
(*"e gli occhi pien d'amor"*) still exists.

He is casting his indifferent glance
upon the tourists with the cameras crowding
the central *piazza*'s fountain
for the predictable, banal adieu.
Taking out the card with Castiglione's portrait
he neatly notes Vassari's phrase:

"So kind and merciful he was
that even the animals loved him."

He would have liked to tell her about him,
to picture for her every detail of his reserved,

reserved in its own anguish, gaze,
as he felt it
the moment it crossed his own.

The painting was hung in the room
that ends in a little retreat—
"*il prezioso gioiello*"—
there, where Federico, just before his eyes were shut,
was studying *On the Sublime*.
He hadn't noticed him the previous time,
as his lust had driven him elsewhere,
to places less lighted, more sensual.
He wanted to,
but he knew that he couldn't.
And, strangely so, his feebleness
to imprint on the paper
all that he saw on that portrait
          (the intelligence especially of his despair)
filled him with joy.

That feebleness was part of the Sublime.
Just like the sun vertically rising in the sky.

New Realism

The perfume burned his eyes, holding tightly to her thighs
and something flickered for a minute and then it vanished
and was gone.
—Lou Reed, "Romeo and Juliette"

He tried to remember the poem
he'd begun to write in silence
on the hotel's verandah with a view to the Aegean.
In vain.
The words had vanished
and along with them had gone
a specific sense of that summer morning.
That morning was as if it had never existed.
It had not existed.

All the previous days
he had been reading Herodotus' *Clio,*
copying excerpts and lines
in the leather-bound notebook given to him
the day they were leaving from Piraeus.
Under the dedication,
in tiny letters,
he had noted the lines:

"Truth is something frightening.
We should not ask for
more than we can handle.
We should not reveal our own truth,
should not force one to accept it,
should not make one want to know things
that transcend human power."

He wished to tell her that the world is always
at the mercy of the mightiest truth,
whether this might defends wisdom
or insanity,
that in the long run truth does not matter,
that everyone has specific limits of sensitivity
beyond which exists neither the true nor the false,
that when Nerval wrote *"Je suis l'inconsolé*
                                    Le prince d'Aquitaine à la tour abolie"

wished to...

but said nothing.
An imaginative dialogue
is not interesting anyway.
He opened the notebook
and on the last page
(where he had just thought of writing a letter)
he painted an olive grove with a cypress in the middle—

the poem of desire
in the poem of the real:

the *chora* of a new realism.

III

Adieu

Apologia Pro Vita Mea

Anatomy of an august night:
devotedly you look
at the poem as it slowly forms the words
(sea   form   reflection)
that will narrate you.

You begin to write:
...the poet is a little figment of imagination
invented in retrospect...
...in the realm of the gaze
distortion prevails...

You stop.
You turn to your side.
She is still lying on the sand;
in her hand, a glass of wine.

...The silent haughtiness
of every man who has deeply suffered
finds all the forms of disguise
necessary
in order to be protected
from contact
with anything that is not
alike in grief...

You have nothing to add.
Maybe one more phrase about *distance* or, rather,
after the dots, about *negation*.

Your eyes are welled with tears.
You are telling a lie
(*sensuality does not point to the other*
but the other's sensuality,
it is the sensuality of sensuality,
the love of the other's love).
You close the notebook.

As you are kissing her
the pawn slides down the snake's tail
and returns to the starting-point—
to darkness.

Sturm Und Drang

...visiting Bachmann in Rome

In the storm of roses
the night is lighted by thorns
and the leaves that formerly lay on the ground in peace
are now screaming under their bare skin,

screaming to welcome
the love that is approaching.

Here,
in this barren land
(the asylum of imagination)
the silent call of nature vibrates,
the secret gift is ripening.

Her enigmatic self-denial
in the winter's solitude
transforms the bare symbols
(the glaring beauty of gazes)
into an eloquent miracle.

With damp promises
the wind
is agitating the foliage of the mind.

(The truth: two bodies
fighting on the moistened ground.)

Descent

And the story has to follow its course
                        to move to the point
                                    where the need

(the need to remember
            to commemorate
                        to claim from the past the most definite
                                    [the most plausible] version)

will wither away
            in resignation
                        (yours?   hers?)
the way a gaze withers away
            the moment when the soul
                        betrayed by the sick body
                                    realises its destination.

Now you wish for the light,
            you wish to speak,
                        to hear your voice spelling her name.

You are standing alone
            in the cool chamber
                        (the poem is flying indifferently
                                    over its etherised interpretations)
waiting for the verdict.

You loved her.
            You must have loved her once.

The years you were confined in the boarding school?
        Earlier?
                When you lived in the *little palazzo* of Cassia Antica?

Once you must have.
        "*Quando la voce del sangue èra...*"
You must.
Even for a while   at the beginning
        or later maybe
                (looking at her wrinkled face
                        behind the barbed wire in Rebibbia)
                                you must have,
    on that wedding trip in Venice
        when you finally saw her in his arms
                (in the arms of the man whom for months
                        she secretly met at the café of Vigna Clara)
or at the moment of the unexpected farewell
        (before the consequences of affect
        [of desertion?]
                became visible)

        yes you must have loved her,
you must have once,
        you must have,
but now you feel nothing.
        Not even pity.
Nothing.
        Only numbness in your feet
                from standing so long.

In a while everything will be over.

You are closing your eyes.

You are visualising yourself in her position.
You are smiling.
This pain relieves you.
...you are departing, leaving behind a world full of words
that belong to you no more...

It's a matter of minutes...

Pietà

1.

the secret was still
resting on the lips—

it then faded
as dreams fade
when the wind begins
to slam the door shutters.

2.

the twig bends,
breaks—

a phrase that
remains incomplete
and lightens the face
with the blush of embarrassment,
of need

(the need to close the eyes,
to let the hands write the epilogue).

3.

when the wind abated
she turned her face to his side,
she smiled,
pulled the sheet softly
up to her eyes

(he caught a glance of the mole
in her right armpit).

4.

there—
at the point where the form is completed
and perfection
(love)
shatters,

there
on the highlands of the scents
where the mandragoras disseminated their aroma.

Pentimento

I was so young, I loved him so, I had
No mother, God forgot me, and I fell.
—Robert Browning, *A Blot in the 'Scutcheon'*

But this is all about her voice.
Any other metaphor would be destined for ruin.
Her voice.
I remove from the setting all the props,
the gestures, the footsteps, the wishful thinking,
for her voice to spread like oil
all over the shattered picture.

The beautiful woman
and her thundering voice.
I can picture this woman
sitting comfortably in her favourite bergére
staring at her interlocutor
with that cunning look of hers
that always knew how to seize
the details of another life
so as to weave its own dreadful imaginings.
I can picture her
seducing the young devotee
with her piercing gaze
that suddenly announces:

Oh, those years in England, blessed are those.
He wanted his thought to move yonder,
he wanted to go farther than all the rest
and naturally farther from us.
Yes, now I can talk about his life.
I am too tired to recapitulate,

but I don't think that he ever lived to be happy.
This child has a knack for grief.
Certainly, there are reasons for that.
Otherwise, it would be a lost cause.
Maybe he is a lost cause.
He has not taken after me.
Not in that at least.
I have made no compromises.
I have been unyielding.
Unyielding.
Easy to say.
Yet words have to be easy
if we want to get somewhere.
The truth is that everything is forgotten.
Both love and lovers
and the dashing gentiluomo.
Everything.
I have always been attracted to adventure, to the paradox.
Now I am unfortunately drowning in monotony,
a woman banished by everyone,
mainly by him.
Yet being up to one's neck in the mire
and not giving in
then at least
you know that the next time
you will do better,
and that there is no next time,
that truly
is a thought for the brave.
The fear of falling leaves me defiant.
Without the fall, there is no vindication.
That was beyond him.
I will never find peace.
Neither will he.

If I could only describe him,
and I know so well how to describe...

Rifts.
There have always been rifts
for the voice ceases,
for the voice pursues,
for the voice cannot come that far,
what difference does it make,
the outcome is the same,
it may make some difference after all,
I may know one day
how to be able to tell,
to finally confess,
the harm I have done
and to whom
and why.

I lived with her.
Kinship means death.
Our only bond
is a painting by Prosalenti,
the Sicilian's porcelain dinner set
—from her third wedding—
and a round onyx table;
nothing, that is.
Every day I would try to write three lines
whose resilience
would transcend mine,
while she, indifferent to what I had preserved,
in the exhalations of familial harmony,
chased the divine Infant
in an Egypt with no god.

Eighteen years at the mercy of that woman.
Eighteen years with the burden of a foreign death.
Oxford was a subterfuge,
the only intelligent move in my life.
Literature, Lawrence's College,
the gothic wit,
all of it an excuse.
The blood contract,
this stifling prohibition
of motherly monstrosity.
This fall has no end.
Retrospection is of no use.
For it is hard to speak
and at the same time focus
on something else,
on what you are truly thinking,
that which is heard in you in whimpers,
in whispers,
as if it is apologising for not being dead.

How strange that a word rubs out the colour
and love, so much love, turns to dust.

Gloriana

...translating Ashbery into Greek

Life—how wonderful it is—
follows our traces
and slowly fades away
in the background of our dreams.

"Of our dreams.
There is always a way
to talk about them
as if their secret meaning
had been revealed to you only,
and yet this *only*
tersely shows
how little it holds."

In the beginning everything seems easy—
almost inevitable.
On a beach, for instance,
with Hardy's poems in her hands,
whispering meaningfully in her ear:

"I have lived with Shades so long,"
and later in the hotel room
after the last embarrassing assurances:
"How tender is this candle...
It bids farewell to the night
drying away its tears."

Is there any point in confessing our pact?
In saying or writing that
"love may be no more

than an exchange of vocabularies",
when the emptiness that befalls us
is already mirrored in the shattered glimmer
                             of our eyes?

The celestial darkness of the book
and the angst of the transparent man
in a translated world.

"Words do not fear words;
they fear the poem."
The end is always the beginning
of a new grandiose disavowal.

Our Face

For Dimitra Christodoulou

It always happens so:
we live between two moments
whose intimacy condemns
every attempt to determine that sensation
still too intense
for us to bury in a recent past
and too faint
for us to drag from a near future.

Yet you continue to exist
in your own self's negative—
a bygone face
imbued by the nostalgia
of another beauty.
The rustling of leaves
(the turning of the page)
brings you back to the place you have chosen
for this refined ritual:
walnut sideboards, Tiffany lights,
Victorian desks…
Your gaze, despite its glaring innocence,
retains the secrecy
of that lost light
which defying the laws of necessity
celebrates that love is here,
guarded in niches unknown to me,
still here, unyielding, unchanged.

The vase is full of chrysanthemums.
This enlightening gesture has no end.
Perhaps an angel looks like what we have not
                                           forgotten.

In Triumph

A paper-thin veil
protects this blazing afternoon
already forsaken by everyone
even by those whose faces
are pictured in the photo so precious to us.

One of them, the one with the naïve smile,
long deceased,
succumbed as his sex ordains
to his own charm;
the other continues to exist
steeped in the whiteness
of its unconditional silence,
an actually two-dimensional reflection
slipping into the dreamy paragon of memory.

If only you could recall the moment
when the two lovers
—for what else could this visual embrace imply—
sacrificed their sensual immortality
to the greed of the lens,
that very second when
the bending of an arm
or the lowering of a gaze
dictated to the eternity of a pose
the story of their common past,
would you perhaps find the words
that bring to life this simple declaration:

that a glossy, embalmed life
is able to perpetuate this passion
in the sighs of the present,

in the glare that forever
enthralls me in your eyes,

            my love.

A Woman with A Past

"A great love harbors
mourning for love" (Oct. 2nd 1989)

…in other words
this story too has come to its end—
just like every story—
and now you're trying with pretentious,
short verses
(such that befit your melodramatic lips)
to save your wounded pride.
Let it be then as you wish.
Let's end it as *poetically* as possible.
(Succinctly, that is.)

I have the gift
to do that much—
the least as you would say—
but which past exactly are you asking me to recall?
Which vows am I to repeat?
I am not judging.
You are judging
in the name of a love that invokes darkness
to return to darkness.

Dreams
do not come true by dreaming.
The enchanted castle is not conquered
with spells of a moment,
nor of course with morbid invocations to the eighth moon.
The return to "normality"
might perhaps be the first step,
just the first step though,

and you appear to have forgotten the rest
or rather to see them as a trite pact.

So stay there.
In your little shelter.
Alone.
Cutting life's deck
and dealing out to absence.

"Dealing out to absence..."
never the last card though,
isn't that so?
That's yours,
you keep it for yourself;
at the crucial moment,
(when the exhausted bodies
will no longer bear to face their nakedness, not even that)
you can raise your hands high
and like a deceived heroine
in *Don Giovanni* cry:
"...the poet has to turn his back on tomorrow
for there is no tomorrow
there is nothing
only our dazed eyes
gazing at our life reflected in the nothing..."

Fine.
Yet, if you knew that this poem
is made out of you
would you write it again
adding everything that I
neglected to say?
Possibly.
Does it matter though?

The bitter taste in the mouth
is not washed away with ardent elegies.
If we are here now,
where even the most refined gesture
appears pretended or redundant,
it's because we have filled our lives with banal,
dazzling words,
words, words, words,
so many words that there's no space left
not even for real sobbing.

We hold the story firmly in our hands—
by all four of its edges.
That's certain.
Come then,
now that there appears in the distance that warm,
worn sun,
let's toss it high in the air
like a white sheet,
again and again,
so every trace of complicit confession,
every scar of pain gets lost.
It's better this way.
The chosen pattern,
still outlined in the wind,
is finally fulfilled
in the deceptive gleam of today.
Who knows
maybe another day
another woman,
a woman-not-spectre,
will recognize in me
her most beautiful face
and love me...

Till then
I will go on
wrenching verses from your rhyming life
and you'll keep dreaming
the arms of a consumptive poet
who writes for you
the new, grand *Ode to Melancholy*.

Closure

1.

The night was falling
            and falling,
the voice talking
kept fading away
until it was completely gone.

Did the lines, I wonder, still exist?
The lines   (that he had written for her)
            outside the voice?

2.

"Not yet and still yes,"
            he responded.
He himself a dream in a dream.

The brightness of the scintillating transparency
no longer invoked the bygone sobs of reality.

The absence has been transformed into
a pure form

an impermeable nakedness of form.

3.

That was the ultimate quietude?
Nothing was calling for him any longer.

Nothing could call for him.

But the voice in the dream…
the already consummated.

(Once upon a time,
he felt it, he must have felt it,
the passion for poetry
the desire to air this invisible breath.)

4.

…for love is a preparation,
expectancy,
a creative presence of mind:
"not yet and still yes".

Then.
Certainly.
In the first éclat
when the need to give shape to its deepest form
still had some meaning.

How about then?

"…a life of erroneous disavowals
untimely farewells,
a life loaded with the dread
of the inevitable despair".

Now that he has reached the limit,
that the adolescent arrogance—
the terrifying arrogance of ignorance—
has disguised as inadequacy
condemned to certain failure?

(Before him
the calm sea stretched to no end
and the secret time of life
was flowing again through his veins.)

5.

"Hang on to me
hang on to me
to hang on to time."

(In the darkness
her hand loomed
to cover his mouth before…)

6.

The bitter
seductive game with words;
always chiselling
again and again.

If only he could
begin again
from the beginning
go back to the summer of 1980

when the poem
still stood
before knowledge.

7.

"Harmony must,
necessarily,
despite everything accomplished
in favour of beauty,
must remain
captive of nothing,
is condemned
to serve the nothing,
for reality avenges life,
has to avenge life
through the poem that celebrates it".

(He knew so
yet he believed that he could
find within its rifts
the definite metaphor of death.)

8.

The end.
Everything has ended.
Gone is that innocence
("so attractive in those years")
that kept him bound to useless knowledge.
Its unmeasured song has died out.

The voice will succumb to the will.
(...they were lying
and through the window were looking silently at the moon
sliding down the black frame.
They knew...)   (so did the night)

IV

A Brazilian Tale

[Poema de dez faces]

For Michael and Edna Longley

I

In my room, the world seems unfathomable.
Yet, when I wander in this strange setting,
I see that it is made of three or four hills,
a beach with palm trees,
and a cloud in the shape of an alligator.
The island is getting ready to welcome the carnival
as I am quietly giving in to her deft hands.

II

With the eye of a gigantic *pernilongo,*
I carefully study the place.
Here the day is spent
on a robust *mulata* slowly taking her clothes off
(unsuspicious of my voluptuous sting)
and a garrulous bartender buying me *caipirinhas* with *maracuja*
to test, as he claims, the *grego*'s limits.

III

João, the young drummer,
consumed with the thrill of *sambodromo,*
(what a word that binds the well-known dance with a parade!)
sleeps under a banana tree in the garden.
The new moon,
a thin sliver of a ripe *manga,*
slowly rises through his dirty hair.

IV

On the beach, the Brazilian attorney of German descent
(the obvious offspring of some *Wehrmacht* lieutenant):
"The Holocaust was
a secular settlement of karma."
Finally, here is a genuinely frigid heart!
From which of the rings of the inferno
has this disgusting *verme* sprung?

V

I walk into the shack where *Joaquim* lives
with his dying father.
"Do you believe in life after death," he asks.
"I do not know. How about you?"
"I cannot say with certainty."
And after a while, clearly answering himself:
"Anyway, God is an over-simplification."

VI

And the color of the sea, like the eyes of the little Christ
who greets me at the entrance of the village with arms wide open.
(At his feet lies a sail with the predictable saying: "Jesus salva").
The summer here either shows its sharp teeth or no longer is.
I taste *guaraná* with the tip of my tongue.
I love this *palavra*. Its flavor returns me to the age
when the name of happiness had one syllable:
you.

VII

Little *Esmeralda* dreams of a villa in Miami—
of lying down under the same, erect palm trees,
of diving into the murky waters of the same ocean,
of eating the same *supermac* with the same pre-fried potatoes,
of dancing *bossa nova* with a rich Cuban,
of finally living like an original American
in the United States of Brazil.

VIII

"The houses with the high ceilings and the Victorian chandeliers
(the mansions of a once English-speaking *senhor*)
watch the white-temple men chase little girls.
If there was more sun, more light,
maybe the passions would have dwindled a little.
But this rain, these drowsy, humid afternoons,
is the devil laughing at our doings, laughing, laughing his head off."

IX

Few books on the shelves in the office.
Among the history of Latin America, Rockefeller's biography
and a guidebook with the Dalai Lama's aphorisms
(with the obvious new age title: *The Art of Happiness*),
I discover a volume of Chekhov's short stories (an English
translation).
I suddenly realise how happy I am to know
that this man has existed.

X

I board the little boat.
As it begins to sail away from the dock,
she loosens her hair scarf
and hurls it into the sea.
"Forsake me," she cries,
"for only then will you remember me once you are away."

(The poem already knows where you hide and binds you
there forever.)

Ilhabela, São Sebastião

NOTES

Pernilongo: a mosquito that can be found in *Ilhabela* (the "beautiful island). The word literally means, "long sting", and its bite is as stinging as the bee's.

Caipirinha: a popular Brazilian drink made of vodka, lime and a little sugar. Many people prefer mango or *maracujá* (a tropical fruit that tastes like passion fruit) to lime. One can make *caipirinha* with *sake* or *pinga*.

Sambodromo: The word literally means, "the road on which all samba schools parade". In reality, it is a long way with rows of seats on both sides, where thousands of spectators are packed to cheer their favorite dancers on.

Verme: worm.

Jesus salva: Christ saves.

Guaraná: the root of a tropical fruit of which they make a popular soft drink.

Palavra: word.

Mina Kiravanta was born in Athens in 1970, studied English
Literature at the Univeristy of Athens and at the State University of
New York (SUNI) at Binghampton, from which she obtained her
Ph. D. in Comparative Literature. She now teaches Critical Theory
and English and American Literature at the University of Athens.

228035LV00001B/3/A

9 781904 556657